One Duck, Another Duck

by CHARLOTTE POMERANTZ
pictures by JOSE ARUEGO and ARIANE DEWEY
Greenwillow Books, New York

For Susan, Thomas, Louie,
and Benjamin —C.P.

For Ada
—J.A. and A.D.

Library of Congress
Cataloging in Publication Data

Pomerantz, Charlotte.
One duck, another duck.
Summary: Danny practices counting
while he and his grandmother watch
first ducks, then swans, swim by.
1. Counting—Fiction.
2. Birds—Fiction.
I. Aruego, Jose, ill.
II. Dewey, Ariane, ill.
III. Title.
PZ7.P77On 1984 [E] 83-20767
ISBN 0-688-03744-5
ISBN 0-688-03745-3 (lib. bdg.)

Danny and his grandmother went to the pond.

They saw a mother duck with her baby ducks behind her. Danny started to count them. "One duck, another duck, another duck, another duck..."

"No," said Grandmother. "You know how to count.
One, two, three, and so on.
Count them again."

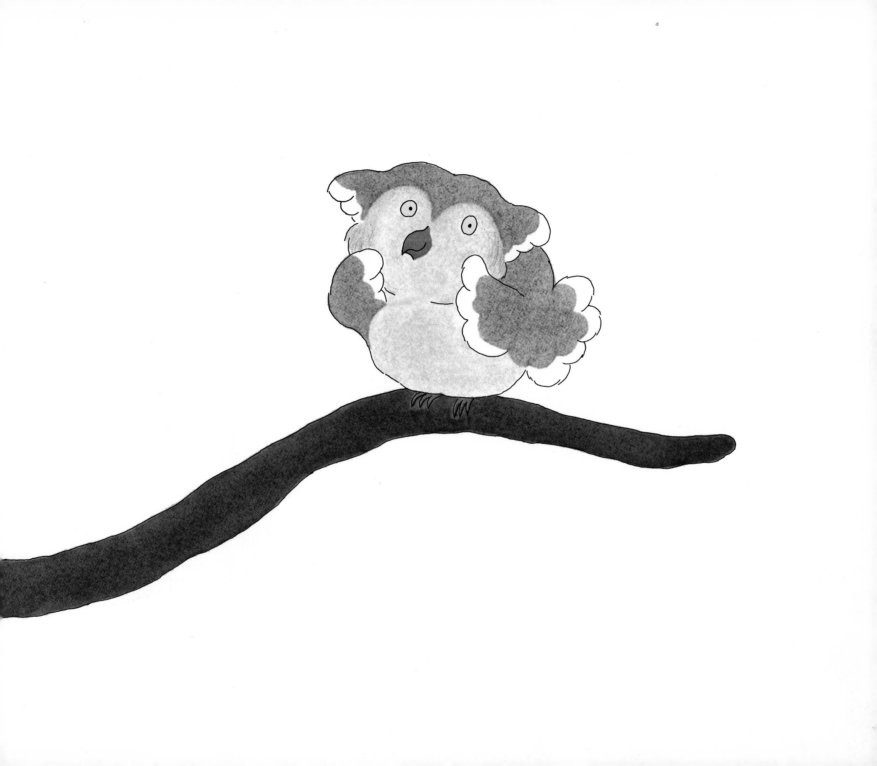

The ducks came out from behind the tall grass. Danny counted. "One duck, another duck...

Two ducks, another duck...

Three ducks, another duck...

Four ducks, another duck...

Five ducks..."

Danny looked and looked.

"Another duck?" he asked.

"No," said Grandmother. "It's a swan.
One swan is not enough to count.
But look...here come some more ducks.
You have counted five.
What comes next?"

Danny counted. "Six ducks, another duck...

Seven ducks, another duck...

Eight ducks, another duck...

Nine ducks," said Danny.

Danny and Grandmother watched the ducks go by.
"Another duck?" he asked.
"No," said Grandmother. "No more ducks."

"Look, Grandma, you are wrong."

"Ten ducks," said Danny. "One, two, three, four, five,
six, seven, eight, nine, ten."
"Very good," said Grandmother.
"You can count to ten."

"Look, Grandma!
    Now there are enough swans to count."

Grandmother yawned.
"No, Danny, enough counting.
It is time to go home."

Danny smiled to himself.
"I know," he thought.
"I'll count the stars."